Power of a Raindrop

Power of a Raindrop

Poetry

Phyllis Moorman

Raven Books
www.ravenbooks.net

Published in the United States of America by
Raven Books
Grand Junction, CO
www.ravenbooks.net

ISBN 978-0-9963990-0-5

Copyright © 2015 by Phyllis Moorman

ALL RIGHTS RESERVED.

Power of a Raindrop

i feel a light tickle as wet drops
   fall from the sky onto my lashes;

i open my mouth to taste the droplets
   as they fall, gentle upon my tongue;

i pause and breathe in the freshness
   surrounding the cleansing rain

and remember that i, too,
   have the power of a raindrop,

the power to change my surroundings,
   to cleanse and refresh my life.

Table of Contents

Nature 1

Statistics are All Wet 1

Last Rose 3

Freedom 4

The Jewels of Fall 5

I Drink to Autumn 6

Mum's the Word 7

The bench I sat on 8

Marshmallow Topping 9

Mother Earth 10

First Kiss of Spring 11

Fading Peach Blossom 12

Ode to the Iris 13

Tweeters and Woofers 14

Early Birds 15

Sunlight 16

Dancing Shadows 17

The Gnarly Old Tree 18

Flowing Waters 20

Finding Peace 21

Inspiration ... 23

Knowing What I Know ... 23

Power of a Raindrop ... 25

Belonging ... 26

Symmetry ... 27

A World Apart ... 28

Following Her Footsteps ... 29

Compassion ... 30

I Can See Clearly Now ... 32

Ode to a Younger Self ... 33

My Garden of Eve ... 34

My Geology ... 36

Open Landing ... 38

Pages of Faded Ink ... 39

Resiliency ... 40

Time Passages ... 42

Trust ... 44

Shut Ins ... 46

Modern-day Warrior ... 47

Half Empty, Half Full? ... 48

Reaching Out ... 49

Do You Believe in Magic? ... 50

My Hands 51
Dancing Through Life 52
Magnetic Attraction 53
My Golden Autumn 54

Nostalgia 55
Let's Walk Together, Mom 55
Golden Hands 57
Blossoming Motherhood 58
Finding My Childhood Home 59
The First Throw 60
He Left, But... 61
Listening to His Rhythm 62
Ivory Keys 63
Old-Fashioned Fun 64
The Skeleton Key 65
Snakeskin 66
Visionary Grandeur 67
Speakers of the House 68
Knitting 70
I shook his hand... 71

Fun 73
Hibernate 73

Bird Talk 75

Clothes 76

Fall's a Mystery 77

Gossip 78

Modern Day Spring Cleaning 79

A Hog to Remember 80

Housewarming Gift Ideas 82

Missing You 83

Never a Free Ride 84

Scraps for Mama LePew 85

The Forbidden Rhyme 86

What goes up, must come down... 87

Nightly Surrender 89

Acknowledgements 91

About the Author 93

Book Description 95

Nature

Statistics are All Wet

"Statistics don't lie," they say.
So kindly explain why I am
drenched by the soaking rain,
when there was only a
10% chance of precip!

Last Rose

The last rose of summer sways precariously
among Fall's lilting warm breezes,
unsure what fate awaits.

Cooler nights crisp the blossom,
browning tips as if creme brûlée,
rounding petals like chocolate curls.

Perfectly timed adaptation,
a delicately freeze-dried beauty,
its essence, forever preserved.

Freedom

Swirling, running, jumping,
      Moving freely among the leaves

Scattering them hither-tither
      Laughing, giggling, smiling

Sharing nature's free spirit
      As only a little boy can.

The Jewels of Fall

Last summer,
thickly clustered emerald leaves,
deflected summer's sun from my face.

Thinned by a changing season,
only a few are left to dangle through
open weaves of twigs and branches;

Yet, as the cooler autumn sun
filters through, they stand out,
sparkling like jewels
of ruby and gold.

I Drink to Autumn

I drink from the cup of autumn,
a mixture of colorfully textured flavors
swirled by cooler breezes in the
ever shortening days of fall.

Mum's the Word

Mum may be
for silence
when planning a surprise,

but

you'll find it
far outspoken
bursting forth
within my yard.

The bench I sat on

in the spring,
allowed me to listen to chirping baby birds;

in the summer,
surrounded me in bursts of happy colors;

in the fall,
enriched me with golden splendor.

Yet, in the winter,
I choose not to sit in its beauty
but to enjoy it from afar.

The cold, white fluff, gently laid
while I slept, is a serenity
I just can't disturb.

Its purity soon enough is breached
as it transforms beneath the sun;
but I'll enjoy the untouched wonder
for as long as I possibly can.

Marshmallow Topping

Marshmallow snow
dips and swags
the lone pine tree
as if an ice cream sundae
awaiting a cherry on top.

Mother Earth

I plant the seeds
in her womb,
knowing she's ready.

I nurture her,
provide for her needs,
protect her from harm,

but only Father Sky can

warm her soil bed,
light the way for her

to birth the
fruits of the earth.

First Kiss of Spring

Sunshine woke me this morning,
teasing me to come touch
dewdrops of fresh rain on the grass,
to play in the puddles that remained.
Ah, the first kiss of spring!

But like all first kisses, it was
quick and non-committal, with a
breeze of a promise of return.

Fading Peach Blossom

As I watch you fade
    from youthful, peachy pink
        past blushing, pale pink
            into a wilting, faded ecru,

I wonder what sweet treasure
your blossom holds.

Ode to the Iris

Oh, tall, stalked beauty of purple plush,

   like a Mexican señorita swirling and
     dancing at her quinceañera,
       celebrating her maturity,

your blossom sways with the breeze,
   a skirt of petals flowing with beauty beneath
     a blouson bodice of scented frills.

Please, do tell...
   Is this *your* quinceañera?

Tweeters and Woofers

Morning speakers,
colorfully feathered
tweeters and woofers,
fill the crisp morning air with
stereophonic music, a great
accompaniment to a daily walk.

Early Birds

I peek out the window,
wondering just what
the chatter is all about
at this early hour.

Rushed, melodic tones
fill the air as a
group of birds
peck at the lawn.

Could it be true—
do only the early birds
get the worms?

Sunlight

Sunlight
Golden splendor
Arise and guide us through
day's color spectrum to Sunset's
orange glow.

Dancing Shadows

Empowered by summer breezes,
shadowy gray images
   mirror the motion of energized trees
   as they dance 'neath the midday sun.

But, like pixies in the forests deep,
they vanish come nightfall,
   disappear into depths unknown.

The Gnarly Old Tree

The gnarly old tree,
weathered and gray,
invited me in
his outstretched limbs.

Comforted by his
lilting breeze, I sat
underneath, entranced
by his charms.

He shared stories
of windswept storms,
though tousled about,
he'd escaped harm.

Pelting rains hadn't
dampened his spirit;
nor had sleet or hail
set off alarms.

Oft briefly burdened
with wet heavy snows,
he took it in stride,
tried to stay warm.

Thoroughly grounded
with support from within,
he embraced all life
with outstretched arms.

Flowing Waters

Mesmerizing plane,
a body of lake water,
aqueous gold of life.

******

Flowing summer streams,
aquatic conversations,
visually sound.

Finding Peace

Perched on an outcropping
of Indian-red sandstone,
I sit still as the birds fly
around and below me,
allowing me the pleasure
to be one with nature,
steeped in its peace,
if only for a little while.

Inspiration

Knowing What I Know

Neophyte I'm not,
but then again;
I've lots to learn ere
wisdom sets in

Power of a Raindrop

i feel a light tickle as wet drops
   fall from the sky onto my lashes;

i open my mouth to taste the droplets
   as they fall, gentle upon my tongue;

i pause and breathe in the freshness
   surrounding the cleansing rain

and remember that i, too,
   have the power of a raindrop,

the power to change my surroundings,
   to cleanse and refresh my life.

Belonging

Sheep stay clustered together,
Lions stay with their pride;

A lost cow will return to the herd,
While joeys don't leave mom's inside.

It's the way it's meant to be,
Being a part of a whole;

So when orphaned very young,
Mother Nature gives a small nudge.

Like when dogs adopt kittens, or
Chimpanzees take to humans;

It fulfills an essential need,
Provides a sense they belong.

Symmetry

A peacock's plume, in full display.
A spider web, radially spun.
Both amazingly symmetrical, and
like a starlet, perceived as beautiful.

A fiddler crab, with a single large claw.
The flounder, with two eyes on top.
True asymmetrical wonders, yet
considered freakish by most standards.

However, like a tree's reflection in the lake,
where the mirrored image differs slightly,
each can be appreciated for its own beauty.

A World Apart

Visually speaking,
I've been all over the world,
seen obvious cultural and
geographical differences;
yet, I am continually struck
by the similarities...

How young seedlings
take roots and grow
into flowers and trees.

How landscapes enhanced
by the setting sun
enthrall young lovers.

How mothers convey affection
without words; tenderness and
loving eyes say it all.

And how people help one
another, without being asked;
benevolent compassion at its best.

It's true our eyes see
how different we are,
but it's the heart that listens
to how similar we are.

Following Her Footsteps

Brightly polished, sun-toasted toes
squish through the sand,
leaving footprints
little girls stretch to walk in,
smiling as they go, trying to
replicate Mom's stride,
eager to follow in her footsteps.

Compassion

Weaving as if
    a chronic drunk,
        he stumbled, the wall catching his fall.
People stared.

I heard revulsion in their whispered voices
    as they turned and walked away.

Not once did they ask if he was okay.
    Not once did they ask if he needed help.
    I guess not many people choose to help a drunk.

My frustration rose to the surface,
    but he remained calm,
        reminding me they don't know him.

He was not drunk nor drugged out.
The long-drawn look on his gaunt face
    can't begin to tell the story of his handicap,
    a mix of post-polio and cerebral palsy,
        slowly taking his body...
            and his life.

It seems today some chose to ignore
    his polio arm, braced leg, and walking stick—
        insignificant in their judgment.

But, he viewed their actions as
                merely a lack of understanding.

Inspired by his capacity for compassion,
       I ask for strength so that I, too, might
            forgive those who misjudge.

I Can See Clearly Now

I never envisioned
a sunset without oranges and reds and yellows.

I never thought blurry vision could be
anything but a view through streaming tears.

And I never dreamed I might not see your smile again
or see the love in your eyes as you look into mine.

However, as we oftentimes do,
I had taken something precious for granted;
I only lost sight of things for a little while,
though I'm sure it was a gift in disguise, for
it helped me refocus my life.

Ode to a Younger Self

I covet the poem I found in the drawer,

For it tells of a young girl,
struggling through youth,
and you can tell by the ink blobs
she didn't stop for fresh pen or paper;
there were thoughts in her mind
she had to write down.

Oh, the impetuousness of youth.
The cryptic cursive didn't do justice
to the legend that followed; at least
it's a legend now, after so many years.

I'd tell you the legend, but
that's not the point. It's just, well,
this scrap of crushed paper
packed and moved many times over
survived it all, just like you or me.

My Garden of Eve

Lush green grass,
accented by royal purple violets,
surrounded by blooms of golden bliss....

Such vibrancy speaks to me,
to come closer so we might
spend the evening together.

With attention of a loving mom,
I fuss over the plants, taking time
to arrange their delicate leaves after
tending their blooms and tendrils.

As so often happens when I'm
absorbed and enjoying myself, though,
the evening passes too quickly
and dusk soon signals its time;

I saunter inside,
sad our evening has to end.

Sighing, I sit by the open window,
enjoying soothing garden scents and
the coolness of the summer eve.

A comfortable softness settles over me;
as if nature is taking care of me,
as I took care of her.

My Geology

I am who I am,
But what am I?

Solidly based but
weathered by time,
Smooth to the touch but
gritty with change.
I am Sandstone.

Cleverly disguised,
accessible to some,
Sparkling gem when
shaped with love.
I am Diamond.

Multifaceted,
both cloudy and clear,
Emanating energy
to those who are near.
I am Crystal.

Subtly unique but
hidden amongst all,
Likenesses overshadow

the glow down below.
I am Gold.

I am who I am,
But what am I?
I'm a multi-faceted woman,
and I'm glad to be me.

Open Landing

Seeds drift
among the breezes,

some landing
stagnantly
on unreceptive soil,

others landing
lively
into fertile ground.

And like ideas floating
freely
in a classroom,

those landing
in a ready core
will take root and grow.

Pages of Faded Ink

Years ago I tore the pages out,
thoughtlessly tossing them aside.
Penned by an impetuous youth,
stories I wished to forget,
experiences I sometimes regretted,
thus forgotten.

Today, the ink returns,
no longer emphatically bold,
but faded. With most details illegible,
visible strokes evince the essence.

Reading between the lines,
I find truths that, with other
experiences, are part of a
larger piece, a work in progress
I call Wisdom.

Resiliency

There's something about
the lonely cactus
barely sticking its head above ground,
thorny spikes forewarning danger,
yet, it still smiles a pink blossom of peace;

and petite wildflowers,
open in pale orange blossoms,
clustered together for protection,
little cups of sweetness in the
stark expanse of the desert.

Just like there's something about people,
the poverty-stricken,
adapting their lifestyle to survive,
or handicapped individuals,
mainstreaming their lives,
or recovered alcoholics or drug addicts,
each day a test of their inner strength.

And, unlike a bungee jumper, bouncing up and down,
energized by the resilient strength of the tethered cord;

the desert flowers and people, struggling to survive,

face the challenges in their lives,
with a resiliency found within themselves,
their ability to bounce back,
an act of *their* strength.

Time Passages

No longer a youthful owner of
Ballerina-style feet or slender hands,
I wear the body of an older woman,
Blessed by passage of time,
Burdened by passage of time.

Wrinkled, arthritic hands hold
In their memory's grasp
Tiny wrinkled babies,
Soft kneaded bread dough,
Rich, warm garden soil,
A lover's gentle hand.

Tired, swollen feet pace
Back to a frenetic time;
Children to and from school,
Me to and from work,
Errands and travel,
Standing in lines.

I choose not to sum up the
Hours I've suffered; for

If time were measured

In pounds, not hours;
My blessings far outweigh
My burdens in life.

Trust

A child holds your hand, and
before she knows it, she's
caught up in the steps and
doesn't realize you've let go, so
easily she goes forward on her own.

And before you know it, she's on a
bicycle, swaying, weaving,
caught up in the forward motion,
determined to ride without training wheels,
evidently unaware when you let go.

And it seems only too quickly, she gives up
bicycling, her third or fourth by now,
caring only to get behind the wheel,
driving with you as her instructor,
each lesson a little easier than the last.

From day one, you were there with her,
growing closer day by day,
her trust of *you* so complete.

It only seems natural,
judging by her successes, that you
know you've been there for her, and that you
love and trust *her* enough to let her go.

Shut Ins

When we close the curtains at night,

Are we trying to shut the world out,
shading ourselves from shadows we don't want to see,
truths we don't want to face, amplified by the night.

Are we like the turtle, retreating inside our shell,
or like the ostrich, hiding our head in the sand,
thinking we're safely concealed against outside forces.

Or are we cocooning, regenerating ourselves
within a peaceful shell of necessary solitude,
emerging as a renewed soul with the dawn's light.

Modern-day Warrior

I stand strong,
a modern-day warrior
posed for peace,
for the spirit dwells within me.

Half Empty, Half Full?

I like traveling the straight-a-way,
enjoying life on an even keel,
like a glass neither empty nor full.

Yet, the view is easily changed,
etched into distortion or
clarified with special lenses.

I can sense when my glass is tilting,
nearing the dreaded half empty.
So, I readjust my perceptual lenses,
and my glass is returned to half full.

Reaching Out

I open my arms wide
to let love reach
my heart.

Do You Believe in Magic?

It could be the way
you kiss me every morning,
how you hold my hand
walking downtown,
or even the way you
ask how I like something...
and then actually remember it.

But it's not.
It's the fact that
you love me enough
to care, to want to please
and to make me happy.

It's not complicated, nor
is there a secret formula
for lasting love. But I do
believe it magic that we
came to find each other.

My Hands

My hands reach out *to touch*...
The smoothness of a flower's petal,
The sharp tip of a thorny bush,
The graininess of sandy soil,
Tickly stubs of fresh-mown grass,

My hands reach out *to feel*...
An associate's firm handshake,
An elder's well-weathered face,
A baby's soft, delicate skin,
My love's comforting embrace.

Dancing Through Life

We no longer rumba or cha-cha
like we did when we were young,

but I find just as much pleasure
hearing your footsteps each morning
as they shuffle across the wooden floor,

your cane keeping time
to your body's rhythmic sway.

Magnetic Attraction

Spinning on the same axis, yet
like the North and South Poles,
we are polarized.

From Eastern and Western culture,
to conservative versus liberal views,
we've formed our own equator.

It's a balance that works,
forming a perfect union as
we encircle our world with love.

My Golden Autumn

I love the season of autumn
where the colors softly change
from greens to autumn hues.

Blessed with warmer days,
refreshed by cooler nights,
these changes are inevitable,
and they'll happen to me and you

as we softly enter our autumn,
the last season of our life,
may we see golden treasures
both old and new alike.

Nostalgia

Let's Walk Together, Mom

> Let's walk together,
> as mentor and friends,
> loving one another
> 'til our time together ends.

Golden Hands

Snuggling 'neath the cozy quilt of
fabric remnants,
I see pieces of my life
threaded together,
and feel the warmth of
Grandma's loving hands.

Blossoming Motherhood

Being a Mother is like a blossoming flower;
it starts slowly, growing hour by hour.
Though budding love for the newborn
is threatened by an occasional thorn,
as the years go by, the petals unfold, and
the love of mothering grows to measures untold.

Finding My Childhood Home

Traveling the country roads
searching for my childhood homes,
helped me realize a home is
more than sticks and stones.

You see, the houses of my youth
have been torn down, replaced
with modern structures
in a nearby space.

Our large country farmhouse
with the white picket fence
represented the American dream,
was home in every sense.

But my favorite memories are not
the color or style of the place;
they are of the times we shared
for those can never be replaced.

The First Throw

Bundled from head to toe,
we waddle out the door,
shouting with excitement
for new-fallen snow.

Gathering snow, then
with mischievous eyes,
he looks all around for
a target to frame.

His little gloved hands
can barely throw, yet
with a giggle and windup,
the ball leaves his fist.

I pretend to duck, but
sway toward the ball;
as the snow flies off me,
I giggle along.

He grins, oh so proud
and the gleam in his eye
brings tears to *my* eyes
as it touches my heart.

He Left, But...

He left, but he didn't leave us.
Memories flood my mind,
flowing so fast at times I
stop to let them absorb me.

I'm reminded how he filled our lives,
how his wisdom seeped throughout,
how his generosity spilled over,
how his love melted our hearts.

I see him when I look in the mirror,
when I watch his children garden,
when I watch the grandchildren play,
or when I look to the clear, blue sky.

Yes, he left, but he didn't leave us.

Listening to His Rhythm

He brought life to the instrument
as his robust breath burst through the
open squares of thin metal and wood.

Cusping the harmonica like a clam,
his hands opened and closed as
melodies vibrated to his rhythm.

Now, his lungs are weak and
I close my eyes and concentrate
on the labored breathing as it
adjusts to an orchestrated rhythm,
a rhythm no longer his own.

Yet, as I listen to the whistle
of oxygen flowing through the tube,
I hear the old melodies as if
the harmonica is still in his hand
and his music once again fills my heart.

Ivory Keys

I blinked through tearful eyes
to see if the yellowed ivory keys
of the old family piano
were really moving.

In my mind's eye, I saw them
dancing a *Sentimental Journey* of
Saturday nights growing up;

a special time when we children
forgot animosity and joined together
in harmony, creating memories
more precious than *Ivory Palaces*.

Old-Fashioned Fun

Buried beneath tools
in a cluttered garage,
lies a childhood sled,
hidden from view.

Twenty-five years since
it was actively used,
our lively five-year-old
set on having fun.

Today the same sled
saw the light of day,
as I tugged and drug
it from beyond its lair.

Our five-year-old grandson,
set on having fun, sledded
the snow-covered hill
our daughter had done.

Hard to imagine
in a techno world,
an old-fashioned toy
could be more fun!

The Skeleton Key

Once dangled from Grandma's keychain,
the spindly shaft with its angled bit
now hangs like a metallic skeleton
at the museum's entrance.

Staring into the case at this rusted old key,
I see through the corrosion from the past
to the strong framework Grandma possessed,
to the doors she opened for others,
to the love she gave from her heart.

I can't help but think this historical piece
not only holds the key to my past
but is the key to my future,
reminding me to open my heart
as she opened hers for me.

Snakeskin

Rocks in the washer,
Snakeskin on the counter,
Socks and shoes scattered,
But none of it mattered.

They were remnants of a child
passing through my life,
and I knew just as certainly
he'd someday be grown and gone.

The house is now like that snakeskin,
a shell of its former life, but
if I could be a snake charmer,
(or perhaps just a lucky Mom),

he'd return with a son, just like himself,
full of fun, mischief (and snakeskins),
and boisterous laughter would again
echo these silenced walls.

Visionary Grandeur

Sixty looked so much older
when my grandmother wore it,
some 50 years before.

Was it the style of her dresses?
She ne'er showed more than ankle
as long dresses were worn back then.

Or was it the way she wore her hair,
braided and rolled in a bun or
permed short, cropped to her ear?

******

I shouldn't compare the view
of this aging, contemporary woman
to my childhood counterpart,
for I now need corrective lenses,
and they distort the vision some.

I think the childhood memories
are the truth as it should be seen:
I see the grandeur of the woman
as viewed from within my heart.

Speakers of the House

Floorboards cry for babies past,
Reminders of sleepless nights,
Pacing till dawn's early light.

Ceilings silence previous bursts
Of jumping, romping youth
Full of energy, having fun.

Walls creak and bellow, a
Reminder of teenage music
Played at full plus volume.

Doors squeak, no longer
Oiled by the young adult,
Trying to enter past curfew.

These sounds of years gone by
Mingle with today's noises, like
Careful, shuffled footsteps,
Daytime nappers' snores, and
Heaters warming old bones.

This house will far outlive us,
But we've left our special mark:

Stories of a life well lived,
Signs of a house well loved.

Knitting

Needles softly click
merging textures and colors;
Heirlooms now emerge.

I shook his hand...

I shook his hand,
and his life coursed through me.

His grip, both rough and callused,
spoke of hard work on the farm,
while the strength throughout his fingers
spoke of courage borne of strife;

The gentleness his second hand
expressed when placed on top,
revealed the caring nature
that he showed to all mankind.

Wrinkled, aged and weathered,
like a much-read, leather book;
these hands depict the story
of my loving Father's life.

Fun

Hibernate

Bears do it,
Snakes do it,
So why, oh why,
Can't I do it!

Bird Talk

Tweets and twitters,
Chittering chatter.
What must they be saying,
and to whom do they speak?

Do robins understand sparrows?
Do doves and owls converse?
Do you think they speak languages
geographically unique?

If a sparrow from down south
would move to the northern shore,
do you think the Southern sparrow
would have an accent and say *y'all*?

Clothes

Hampered,
they seem abundant;

closeted,
but few.

Fall's a Mystery
(Or I've Been Watching Too Much Crime TV)

Blustery winds bring seasonal mysteries, like
why once supple flowers turn crispy and still,
why leaves lose color and fall dead away,
why summer's loud bugs turn eerily quiet,
and why some people fade when the sun disappears.

If I were a detective, I'd capture the flowers
and confine them indoors for, say, 90 days,
after which, if warm, they'd be returned outdoors.

I'd turn the leaves over to the homicide folks
and hope an autopsy could reveal why
once green and pliant, they're now crunchy and brown;

I'd send my partner on a seasonal stakeout
along with a sensitized listening device
to determine if crickets have Winter sounds;

And for the people, if they'd consider a change,
I'd see them moved to a sunnier place,
and as their sponsor, of course I'd move, too.

Gossip

Conversations with gossips are
like a drop of ink on a coffee filter;
the juicier it is, the faster it spreads.

Modern Day Spring Cleaning

Hours I used to spend cleaning
bed springs,
closets, attics and such,

I now spend updating, syncing,
adding, deleting...
with but a single touch.

Whereas I battled heavy lifting,
I now merely sit,
moving very little of my body;

just a finger tapping,
instructing electronic gadgets
to clean or scrub the stuff.

A Hog to Remember

My cousin rode a hog one day
but it can't begin to compare
to the hog I saw my grandma on,
the one she rode with flair.

It started at my uncle's house;
The family was gathered there.
My uncle got to bragging about,
Then Grandma he did dare.

He said, "Come ride my hog with me;
It's unique and rather rare."
"I can't," she most demurely said,
"I just can't muss my hair."

He begged, "Just once around the yard,
We'll ride slowly as a mare."
Always one to join the fun,
she said, "I'll be right there."

Now we grandkids got excited
but we warned her, "Please beware,
for Uncle tends to drive real fast
and end up who knows where."

He hopped upon his metal hog,
a motorcycle most fair;
And Grandma sat behind him---
indeed, they were quite the pair.

He loudly revved the engine up
She excitedly waved the air;
Then grinning ear to ear and beyond,
'round the yard they rode with care.

Grandma giggled, I giggled along
till I nearly fell out of my chair;
But I'll always remember my Grandma,
for no one can compare.

Housewarming Gift Ideas

Excitement of a new home
dwarfed by wobbly knees,
tired, crooked back,
dangling, strained arms.
Sound familiar?

If anybody's listening, I'd like
to suggest any housewarming gift
be held to things that don't need
assembled, put on display or hung.

Just slip a gift certificate to a
nearby masseuse inside an envelope
with sincere wishes for a speedy recovery...
And did I mention I like chocolate and wine?

Sincerely yours,

Missing You

Staring pensively,
I keep watching
for you to come home.
I can't remember how long
you've been gone,
but I miss you so.

I'm sure sitting listlessly
won't bring you back
any sooner, but
I just can't seem to focus
on anything but you.

We have such fun
when we're together,
and I get so lonely
when you're not here.

May wishing you here,
make it so.

                Lovingly,

                Fido

Never a Free Ride

Beautiful little oxpecker*
atop the rhinoceros;

why does he not protest
as you perch upon his back?

Do you tickle his fancy as
you clean bugs from his skin;

Or are meals and transport,
reward for warnings
of dangers far and near?

No matter the rhyme or reason
of why you co-exist,
You bear homage to the adage,
"There are no free rides anywhere."

*oxpeckers are the birds that ride on a rhinoceros's back.

Scraps for Mama LePew

Bundled in an old woolen scarf and coat,
Mama braved the winter's chill and dark of night,
headed to the yard's section most remote.

A ten-foot pole cast a small beam of light
upon the ground where the dog's scrap dish sat,
our remains to become the dog's delight.

Not having looked up, she didn't see the cat—
The one with the stripe running down its back!
And look at the babies the cat had begat!

Mama Skunk was kind, she did not attack.
My mama, running hard, was nearly aflight —
Food was strung all along the return track!

Now we wish not to cause Mama another such fright,
So we chill all our dog scraps, they must wait overnight.

The Forbidden Rhyme

If now heard on playgrounds,
they'd surely be expelled,

Cinderella kissing boys;
robbers hanging 'round;

The familiar playground jingles
we recited as we jumped,

just don't set an image
today's teachers will allow.

What goes up, must come down...

Balls,
Balloons,
Teeter totters,
Skydivers,
High tide,
My weight.

Nightly Surrender

I surrender to you,

Goddess of Slumber,

may the night's sleep

bring dreams to remember.

Acknowledgements

Many thanks to the editors of the following publications in which some of the poems first appeared.

Colorado Journeys, "Sunlight"

Western Colorado Writers' Forum section of *The Daily Sentinel*, "Finding Peace" and "Pages of Faded Ink"

Grand Valley Magazine, "The First Throw"

About the Author

Phyllis Moorman lives in the gorgeous yet diverse expanse of Western Colorado. She has authored five books of poetry, has been published in a number of newspapers and magazines and shares her poetry on her blog and website.

Book Description

From snow-capped mountains to the rocky desert, Nature has never been described better. Thoughts on love, joy, and challenges in life are thought-provoking pearls you'll visit over and over again. Join the poetic journey to see if you, too, possess the **Power of a Raindrop.***

*Signature poem: page 25

www.ingramcontent.com/pod-product-compliance
Lightning Source LLC
Chambersburg PA
CBHW031425290426
44110CB00011B/534